Without Excuse: Principles of God's Judgment

Without Excuse: Principles of God's Judgment

by
John MacArthur, Jr.

"GRACE TO YOU"
P.O. Box 4000
Panorama City, CA 91412

ISBN: 0-8024-5321-X

1 2 3 4 5 6 Printing/LC/Year 94 93 92 91 90

Printed in the United States of America

Contents

These Bible studies are taken from messages delivered by Pastor-Teacher John MacArthur, Jr., at Grace Community Church in Panorama City, California. These messages have been combined into a 4-tape album titled *Without Excuse: Principles of God's Judgment*. You may purchase this series either in an attractive vinyl cassette album or as individual cassettes. To purchase these tapes, request the album *Without Excuse: Principles of God's Judgment*, or ask for the tapes by their individual GC numbers. Please consult the current price list; then, send your order, making your check payable to:

The Master's Communication
P.O. Box 4000
Panorama City, CA 91412

Or call the following toll-free number:
1-800-55-GRACE

1
Principles of God's Judgment—Part 1

Outline

Introduction
- A. Identifying the Moralist
- B. Exposing the Moralist
  1. The Gentile
  2. The Jew
     - *a*) Salvation by nation
     - *b*) Salvation by covenant

Lesson
- I. Knowledge (v. 1)
  - A. The Implication
    1. Knowledge through natural revelation
    2. Knowledge through conscience
    3. Knowledge through the law of God
  - B. The Identification
  - C. The Condemnation
    1. The proof
    2. The practice
- II. Truth (vv. 2-3)
  - A. Righteous Judgment (v. 2)
  - B. Personal Application (v. 3)
    1. The intensity
    2. The indictment
    3. The implications

Conclusion

Introduction

In Romans 1:18-32 the apostle Paul paints a striking picture of evil, debauched men and women. They've abandoned God, so God abandons them to the consequences of their sin.

A. Identifying the Moralist

However, at the end of Romans 1 a very important question remains unanswered: what about good people? What about those who aren't murderers, liars, thieves, fornicators, adulterers, and homosexuals? What happens to the people who haven't abandoned all sense of right and wrong?

In this world are people who do not appear to be idolatrous or sinful—they may even identify with true religion. In Paul's day those people were the Jews. In our day they are professing Christians who want to uphold the moral standards of Scripture. But those who are not true believers are unable to maintain an external moral value system because they cannot restrain their own sinfulness. In essence they cover their darkened hearts with cloaks of light.

B. Exposing the Moralist

In Romans 2 Paul exposes the moralist. The moralist agrees with Paul's condemnation of the idolaters in chapter 1 because he sees himself as better than they and therefore uncondemned. But that attitude produces a false sense of security. In Romans 3:19 Paul says, "We know that whatever things the law saith, it saith to them who are under the law, that every mouth may be stopped, and all the world may become guilty before God." A person understands the Christian gospel only when he recognizes that he is guilty before God—whether he is immoral (chapter 1) or moral (chapter 2), whether Gentile (chapter 1) or Jew (chapter 2).

1. The Gentile

In Romans 2 Paul may have been referring to a person who may not adhere to any particular religion but thinks he's moral because he upholds a moral, ethical code of living.

2. The Jew

It is most likely that Paul had the Jews in mind when he wrote this passage. They would certainly have agreed with Paul's condemnation of the Gentile world, believing themselves exempt from judgment. The Jews, taking their lead from the prophet Jonah, traditionally believed that God would destroy the Gentiles because of their sin. If Jonah had had his way, he would have wiped out all the Ninevehs of this world.

a) Salvation by nation

Because of both their physical and religious identification with Israel, the Jewish people assumed they were exempt from God's judgment. They were the chosen people. They expected to be regarded and treated not as individuals but as a nation. They thought there was no consequence to their personal sin because they believed they were under a national salvation.

b) Salvation by covenant

They also believed in salvation by their covenant—a belief we now call sacramentalism. Because they were circumcised on the eighth day and adhered to other such sacraments, they believed they were in the covenant.

That basic thinking is prevalent in many Protestant churches today. For example, if a child is baptized as an infant, that sacramental act allows him entrance into the covenant. He is then confirmed when he is twelve. Those sacraments supposedly guarantee that the child will have a place in God's kingdom and will not be condemned with the rest of the world.

Thus the Jews believed that their adherence to the traditions and their sacramental attachment to the covenant exempted them from judgment. Many people hold similar beliefs today. They get baptized, they go to church, they keep the rules, and they lead moral lives. But they're self-righteous. They don't think they will ever be judged. And they are the hardest people to reach with the gospel—much harder than reprobates who have hit bottom and have no other options.

With great force and clarity Paul points out that the ethical, moral person who does not know Christ—whether Jew or Gentile—will find himself in the same hell as a pagan idolater. If the Gentile is without excuse, then the Jew is even more to blame because he had more information at his disposal. Paul wanted the religious person who had outwardly identified himself with Judaism (or Christianity in today's terms) to know he wouldn't escape judgment.

Lesson

We see six principles of judgment in Romans 2:1-16. God judges all men and women on the basis of knowledge, truth, guilt, deeds, impartiality, and motives.

I. KNOWLEDGE (v. 1)

"Therefore, thou art inexcusable, O man, whosoever thou art that judgest; for wherein thou judgest another, thou condemnest thyself; for thou that judgest doest the same things."

A. The Implication

"Therefore" connects what Paul is going to say with what he said in the previous chapter. What was true of the people implicated in Romans 1:18-32 is also true of this new group. They are without excuse.

Romans 1:18-19 says, "The wrath of God is revealed from heaven against all ungodliness and unrighteousness of men who hold the truth in unrighteousness, because that which may be known of God is manifest in them." So verse

20 says they are without excuse. Thus when Romans 2:1 says, "Therefore, thou art inexcusable, O man," the implication is that his readers also know the truth.

They prove they know the truth because they judge others. If they have a criterion with which to judge others, they must know the truth and are therefore inexcusable.

1. Knowledge through natural revelation

   It was clear that the Gentiles knew the truth through natural revelation—the obvious existence of God as seen in all creation—from what Paul said in Romans 1:19-20. Likewise the Jewish people knew the truth, according to chapter 2.

2. Knowledge through conscience

   Romans 2:14 says, "The Gentiles, who have not the law, do by nature the things contained in the law." Both Jews and Gentiles have an innate knowledge of right and wrong via the conscience.

3. Knowledge through the law of God

   a) Romans 3:1-2—"What advantage, then, hath the Jew? Or what profit is there of circumcision? Much every way, chiefly because unto them were committed the oracles of God." The Jewish people had the truth of God in written form. Therefore they were just as inexcusable—if not more inexcusable—as the Gentiles, for they not only had the light of nature and conscience but also the revealed Word of God.

   b) Romans 9:4-5—"[To the] Israelites . . . pertaineth the adoption, and the glory, and the covenants, and the giving of the law, and the service of God, and the promises; whose are the fathers, and of whom, as concerning the flesh, Christ came." They had all the benefits and all the revelation, so they were without excuse.

B. The Identification

The phrase "O man" (cf. Rom. 2:3; 9:20) is a general reference to any moralist who thinks he's exempt from judgment because he hasn't sunk to idolatry, homosexuality, or other reprobate activity.

Paul says the man of Romans 2 is inexcusable because he had knowledge. In fact, he had a more complete knowledge, so he was even more inexcusable. Some of the Jews of Paul's day who would have read this chapter knew all about Christ yet rejected Him. That relegated them to the status described in Hebrews 10:29: "Of how much sorer punishment, suppose ye, shall he be thought worthy, who hath trodden under foot the Son of God, and hath counted the blood of the covenant, with which he was sanctified, an unholy thing?"

"Whosoever thou art that judgest" (Rom. 2:1) indicates that the moralist knew God's standards since he applied them to someone else. Anyone who sits in the seat of moral judgment and condemns others for their sin proves that he himself is inexcusable. Romans 1:32 says that even pagans know "the judgment of God, that they who commit such things are worthy of death." Even pagans know what is right and wrong. The moralist is like a judge who condemns a criminal by applying the law—in so doing he himself becomes responsible to keep that law.

C. The Condemnation

1. The proof

In Romans 2:1 Paul says to the moralist, "Wherein thou judgest another, thou condemnest thyself." He was restating what our Lord said in Matthew 7:1: "Judge not, that ye be not judged." That doesn't mean we shouldn't properly evaluate things. In verses 15-20 Jesus says we're to examine the fruit of those who claim to speak for God. But in verse 1 Jesus tells us to stop criticizing and condemning people. Stop finding fault with others. Stop being self-righteous. Stop impugning people's motives when you cannot possibly read their hearts. Stop pushing your criticism to the point that you play God.

In verse 2 Jesus says, "With what judgment ye judge, ye shall be judged; and with what measure ye measure, it shall be measured to you again." That's why James 3:1 says, "Be not many teachers, knowing that we shall receive the greater judgment." Why is a teacher's condemnation greater than the rest of mankind? Because the more a man knows, the more greatly he is condemned if he doesn't act in accordance with his knowledge. The Lord went on to teach that before you try to remove the splinter from your brother's eye, you had better get the two-by-four out of your own eye (Matt. 7:3-5). It's a fatal human tendency to exaggerate the faults of others and minimize our own.

2. The practice

Why do the judgments of moralists result in their own condemnation? Romans 2:1 says, "Thou that judgest doest the same things." The moralist claims he doesn't do the things the pagan does. He claims he doesn't commit the same sins—that he's a moral man who keeps the law of God. Like the rich young ruler he says, "All these things [the Ten Commandments] have I kept from my youth up" (Matt. 19:20). What an illusion!

a) Matthew 5:21-22—Jesus said, "Ye have heard that it was said by them of old [your rabbis taught you], Thou shalt not kill and whosoever shall kill shall be in danger of judgment; but I say unto you that whosoever is angry with his brother without a cause shall be in danger of judgment; and whosoever shall say to his brother, Raca, shall be in danger of the council; but whosoever shall say, Thou fool, shall be in danger of hell fire." The moralists our Lord addressed had not actually murdered, but they killed people in their hearts. They refrained from actual murder because they sought to be respected and regarded as righteous. But within their hearts they were murderers. False religion cannot restrain sin in the heart, although it can mask it with self-righteousness.

b) Matthew 5:27-28—"Ye have heard that it was said by them of old, Thou shalt not commit adultery; but I say unto you that whosoever looketh on a woman to lust after her hath committed adultery already in his heart."

c) Matthew 5:31-32—They also committed adultery through divorce. When these moralists wanted to commit adultery, they divorced their current spouses and married other women, supposedly legalizing their adultery.

d) Matthew 5:33—"Again, ye have heard that it hath been said by them of old, Thou shalt not perjure thyself, but shalt perform unto the Lord thine oaths." People offered oaths continually to impress others with their sincerity. But as long as they swore by something other than God, they believed they didn't have to fulfill their oath. For example, if someone swore by heaven to pay a debt but then reneged on it, he could say he didn't make the oath to God so he didn't have to honor it. Although they took oaths to fulfill the rabbinic traditions, they were liars at heart.

e) Matthew 5:38—"Ye have heard that it hath been said, An eye for an eye, and a tooth for a tooth." Essentially the rabbis were establishing vengeance as every man's God-given right according to the law of Moses. But that statement was originally for use in the law courts to insure proper punishment for a crime. It had nothing to do with personal vengeance. Jesus said, "Resist not evil, but whosoever shall smite thee on thy right cheek, turn to him the other also" (v. 39).

Self-righteous people make two fatal mistakes: they misunderstand the breadth of God's law, which encompasses the internal man, and they misunderstand the depth of their sin. Our Lord's logic is clear and convincing. Those who condemn others prove that they know the law. But because of that knowledge they condemn themselves, for they do the same things of which they condemn others. The same conscience that allows one to recognize wrong in others brings condemnation upon the moralist.

Romans 2 makes clear that the moralist is just as bad as everyone else; he just happens to be able to cover up his sin. He who claims that he is moral and religious because he's basically good, goes to church, and has been baptized may only be restraining the flesh externally. Internally he may be full of unrestrained evil. And he will be judged for that.

II. TRUTH (vv. 2-3)

A. Righteous Judgment (v. 2)

"We are sure that the judgment of God is according to truth against them who commit such things."

"Such things" refers to the evils mentioned in chapter 1. "We are sure [Gk., *oidamen*]" reveals that it is an obvious, basic principle that the judgment of God is according to truth. Why? Because God cannot lie (Titus 1:2). God is truth—that is His nature.

1. Genesis 18:25—"Shall not the Judge of all the earth do right?" We will be judged according to the truth.

2. Romans 3:4—"Let God be true, but every man a liar." It is God's nature to be true, and He will judge everything with truth.

3. Romans 9:14—Paul says, "Is there unrighteousness with God? God forbid." God never makes any evaluation or takes any action that is not correct.

4. Psalm 9:4, 8—"Thou hast maintained my right and my cause; thou didst sit on the throne judging right. . . . and he shall judge the world in righteousness."

5. Psalm 96:13—"For [the Lord] cometh to judge the earth; he shall judge the world with righteousness, and the peoples with his truth." Our perception is often distorted, but not God's.

6. Psalm 145:17—"The Lord is righteous in all his ways, and holy in all his works." That refers to His works of judgment in addition to His other works.

7. Isaiah 45:19—"I have not spoken in secret, in a dark place of the earth. I said not unto the seed of Jacob, Seek

ye me in vain; I, the Lord, speak righteousness, I declare things that are right."

Abusing God's Grace

We all tend to exonerate ourselves. We say, "God would never judge me," "I'm basically a good person," or, "It will all be all right in the end." We are so used to God's mercy that we take it for granted. Since God doesn't strike us dead as soon as we sin, we think we will never be punished for wrongdoing. Yet the Bible says that the wages of sin is death (Rom. 6:23). Every time you sin God has a perfect right to snuff out your life. We abuse His mercy instead of being grateful for His graciousness.

8. 1 Corinthians 4:3—Paul says, "With me it is a very small thing that I should be judged of you, or of man's judgment; yea, I judge not mine own self." He was not at all concerned about how others judged him because he was well aware that man's judgment is hopelessly distorted. Then he says, "I know nothing against myself; yet am I not hereby justified; but he that judgeth me is the Lord. Therefore, judge nothing before the time, until the Lord come, who both will bring to light the hidden things of darkness, and will make manifest the counsels of the hearts" (vv. 4-5). Man's judgment does not square with the facts, but God's does. The problem with the moralist is that he thinks he is righteous because he judges himself by his own standards.

9. Hebrews 4:13—"Neither is there any creature that is not manifest in his sight, but all things are naked and opened unto the eyes of him with whom we have to do." Every sin you have ever committed might just as well have been played on a full-sized screen in front of God. Every evil thought, word, or deed has been committed in His presence. Although we know He hates sin, we continue to sin in front of Him. The writer of Hebrews said, "Seeing, then, that we have a great high priest . . . Jesus, the Son of God, let us . . . come boldly" (vv. 14, 16). If we understand that we are constantly exposed to God, we had better run to the One who can

mediate between us and the most high Judge—the Lord Jesus.

God's judgment is not predicated on outward appearance or profession but on truth. The hypocrite hopes that God will judge him by something other than the truth. He hides behind his national identity, church affiliation, baptism, adherence to rules, or morality. Whereas man looks at the outward appearance, God looks at the heart (1 Sam. 16:7). Today many people who go to church—whether they're Lutheran, Presbyterian, Baptist, Catholic, Episcopalian, or any other denomination—think they will escape God's judgment, while at the same time they sit in judgment of the immoral world. In their hearts, however, they are full of the same immorality. They're like whited sepulchers: washed clean on the outside but inside full of dead men's bones (Matt. 23:27).

B. Personal Application (v. 3)

"Thinkest thou this, O man, that judgest them who do such things, and doest the same, that thou shalt escape the judgment of God?"

1. The intensity

The Greek word translated "thinkest" (*logizomai*) means "to estimate" or "calculate." The intensity of verse 3 is lost in our English translation. In his commentary on this verse Donald Grey Barnhouse paraphrased it thus: "You dummy—do you really figure that you have doped out an angle that will let you go up against God and get away with it? You don't have a ghost of a chance." Then Barnhouse said, "There is no escape. Do you understand? No escape—ever. And this means you—the respectable person, sitting in judgment upon another fellow creature, and remaining unrepentant yourself" (*God's Wrath: Romans 2:1–3:20* [Grand Rapids: Eerdmans, 1953], p. 18).

2. The indictment

Verse 3 tells us that the moralist cannot avoid being judged and that when he is judged, he will not be able to avoid being condemned. When he is condemned he will not be able to avoid being executed.

3. The implications

a) 1 John 3:20—"If our heart condemn us, God is greater than our heart, and knoweth all things." God has built within us a conscience. It is like pain. Pain calls you to a halt when your body is injured. Your conscience calls you to a halt when your soul is injured. Though we are fallen, our conscience condemns us; can you imagine how greatly God, who is unfallen and eternally and infinitely holy, condemns us?

b) Hebrews 12:25-29—"See that ye refuse not him that speaketh. For if they escaped not who refused him that spoke on earth, much more shall not we escape, if we turn away from him that speaketh from heaven, whose voice then shook the earth; but now he hath promised, saying, Yet once more I shake not the earth only, but also heaven. And this word, Yet once more, signifieth the removing of those things that are shaken, as of things that are made, that those things which cannot be shaken may remain. Wherefore, receiving a kingdom which cannot be moved, let us have grace, by which we may serve God acceptably with reverence and godly fear; for our God is a consuming fire."

That is a comparison to Israel at Mount Sinai. The Israelites didn't escape when they refused to hear the voice of God that thundered out of the mountain. That entire generation died in the wilderness. If they didn't escape when God spoke on earth, do you suppose anyone will escape when he or she refuses to listen to God speak the gospel from heaven? How much greater the judgment will be when God speaks from a heavenly throne than when He spoke from an earthly mountain.

c) Hebrews 2:2-3—"If the word [the Mosaic law given at Sinai] spoken by angels was steadfast, and every transgression and disobedience received a just recompense of reward, how shall we escape, if we neglect so great salvation, which at the first began to be spoken by the Lord?" Since people were judged for denying a law spoken by angels, how much more will we be judged for denying a law spoken by Christ Himself!

Conclusion

God knows everything about us, but the people around us don't. They may know some details about us, but no one can know everything. We don't even know our own innermost motives, and we're hopelessly biased in our own favor anyway. However, each of us will be judged according to the truth and our knowledge of God.

If you know you're not right with God—that you're playing a religious game and condemning sin in others while it's also boiling within you—you need to run to Jesus Christ. He has already paid the penalty. He has already received the judgment of God on your behalf.

Satisfying Love and Law

Tribes once roamed the Soviet expanse much like Indian tribes roamed the Americas. The tribes that controlled the best hunting grounds and the choicest natural resources had the strongest and wisest leaders. I heard about one particular tribe whose success was due to the fairness and wisdom of the laws that their great leader made and enforced. His word was law. One of his greatest laws was that parents must be loved and honored. Other laws stated that murder was punishable by death and that stealing required severe punishment.

The tribe was prospering greatly when something disturbing began to occur. Someone in the tribe began stealing. It was reported to the great leader. He sent out a proclamation that when the thief was caught, he would receive ten lashes from the tribal whip master. The thievery continued despite the warning, so he raised the punishment to twenty lashes. Still it continued, so he increased it to thirty. Finally he raised it to forty. He knew that only one person in the tribe could survive such a severe lashing—himself.

Eventually the thief was caught. To everyone's horror, it was the great leader's own aged mother. The people wondered what the leader would do. His law said that parents were to be loved and honored, yet thieves were to be whipped. Great arguments arose as the day of judgment approached. Would he satisfy his love and save his mother, or would he satisfy his law and watch his mother die under the whip? Soon tribal members were divided—they even bet on what he would do.

Finally the day came. The tribe gathered around the great compound. In the center a large post was driven into the ground. The leader's great throne sat in the place of prominence. With great pomp and ceremony the leader entered and took his place on the throne. The silence was deafening. His frail little mother was led into the compound between two towering warriors. They tied her to the post. The crowd murmured in debate: will he satisfy his love at the expense of his law, or his law at the expense of his love? The tribal whip master entered carrying a long leather whip. He was a powerful man with bulging muscles. As he approached the little woman, the warriors ripped her shirt off, exposing her frail little back to the cruelty of the lash. Everyone gasped. Was the leader really going to let her die?

The leader sat staring without moving. All eyes darted from him to the whip master and back again. The whip master took his stance, and his great arm cracked the whip in the air as he prepared to bring the first lash down upon her.

Just as the whip master brought his powerful arm forward with the first cutting stroke, the leader held up his hand to halt the punishment. A sigh of relief went up from the tribe. His love would be satisfied. But what about his law?

The leader rose from his throne and strode toward his mother. As he walked, he removed his own shirt, throwing it aside. He then wrapped his great arms around his mother, exposing his muscular back to the whip master. Breaking the heavy silence he commanded, "Proceed with the punishment." Both his law and his love were satisfied.

Romans 6:23 says, "The wages of sin is death." Jesus wrapped His arms around you. He satisfied His love, for He enabled us to escape God's wrath. He satisfied His law, for He paid the penalty for sin. That's the genius of God and the gift of salvation.

Focusing on the Facts

1. Who are the people who identify with God yet are not true believers (see p. 8)?
2. Why did most of the Jewish people believe they were saved? Explain (see p. 9).
3. Explain how Paul uses information from Romans 1:18-32 to explain what he says in Romans 2 (see pp. 8-10).
4. In what three ways does the moralist prove he has knowledge of God (see p. 10)?
5. Why was the Jew especially inexcusable (see p. 11)?
6. Explain the phrase "whosoever thou art that judgest" (Rom. 2:1; see p. 12).
7. What teaching of Jesus is Paul reiterating in Romans 2:1? Explain it (see pp. 12-13).
8. Why does the moralist's judgment result in his own condemnation (Rom. 2:1; see p. 13)?
9. Give scriptural examples of people who claimed to keep the law but in reality didn't (see pp. 13-14).
10. What basic principle is true regarding the judgment of God? Support your answer with Scripture (see pp. 15-16).
11. What do we tend to do regarding God's grace? Explain (see p. 16).
12. Why was Paul unconcerned about how others judged him (1 Cor. 4:3-5; see p. 16)?
13. What should be our response when we realize our sin is exposed to God (Heb. 4:16; see pp. 16-17)?
14. What is the hypocrite's hope (see p. 17)?
15. According to Donald Barnhouse, what is one way to paraphrase Romans 2:3 (see p. 17)?
16. What does Romans 2:3 tell us about the moralist (see pp. 17-18)?
17. How is our conscience like pain (1 John 3:20; see p. 18)?

Pondering the Principles

1. Are you in the habit of being obedient externally but ignoring your internal state? Read Matthew 5:21-48. Have any of those sins become characteristic of you? Which ones? To bring your thoughts into the captivity of Christ (2 Cor. 10:4-5), you need to be studying God's Word daily. Discipline your mind to focus on Christ so that your natural responses are godly and not fleshly.

2. Have you ever taken God's grace for granted? Give some examples of times that you have. Why do you suppose we who have been forgiven so much can forget what God has done? Make a list of things that have happened to you in the past where you could see God's grace at work. Now thank Him for His abundant grace. Begin to examine the events of each day and identify the evidence of God's grace in your life.

2
Principles of God's Judgment—Part 2

Outline

Review

I. Knowledge (v. 1)

II. Truth (vv. 2-3)
  - A. Righteous Judgment (v. 2)
  - B. Personal Application (v. 3)

Lesson

III. Guilt (vv. 4-5)
  - A. God's Goodness (v. 4)
    1. The devaluation of His goodness
    2. The depth of His goodness
       - *a*) "Goodness"
       - *b*) "Forbearance"
       - *c*) "Long-suffering"
    3. The demonstration of His goodness
       - *a*) As seen in the psalms
       - *b*) As seen in the world
         - (1) The past
         - (2) The present
    4. The design of His goodness
       - *a*) Inspected
       - *b*) Rejected
  - B. Ultimate Judgment (v. 5)
    1. The problem
       - *a*) How people view themselves
       - *b*) How people view God
         - (1) The wrong perspective
           - (*a*) Lot's wife
           - (*b*) The Canaanites
           - (*c*) Aaron's sons

(*d*) The Flood
(*e*) Capital punishment
(2) The right perspective
(*a*) God's original penalty was just
(*b*) God was merciful
(*c*) God has a right to judge
2. The result
a) The state of the heart
b) The time of the judgment

Conclusion

Review

In Romans 2:1-16 Paul establishes the basis of judgment that applies to everyone. Most particularly he focuses on the outwardly moral and religious person who saw himself as better than the reprobates referred to in chapter 1. We learn that God judges according to knowledge, truth, guilt, deeds, impartiality, and motive.

I. KNOWLEDGE (v. 1; see pp. 10-15)

"Therefore, thou art inexcusable, O man, whosoever thou art that judgest; for wherein thou judgest another, thou condemnest thyself; for thou that judgest doest the same things."

II. TRUTH (vv. 2-3)

A. Righteous Judgment (v. 2; see pp. 15-17)

"We are sure that the judgment of God is according to truth against them who commit such things."

B. Personal Application (v. 3; see pp. 17-19)

"Thinkest thou this, O man, that judgest them who do such things, and doest the same, that thou shalt escape the judgment of God?"

That is characteristic of those who say to the Lord that they've done many good things in His name (Matt. 7:22). Their claim is just a facade of religious externals. Jesus will say to such people, "I never knew you; depart from me" (v. 23). First Thessalonians 5:3 expresses the same thought: "When they shall say, Peace and safety, then sudden destruction cometh upon them." Man thinks he is secure until the judgment of God comes like a thunderbolt. Then there will be no escape. God keeps a perfect record of the thoughts, words, and deeds of every human being. That is the data by which God renders the ultimate verdict in divine judgment.

Lesson

III. GUILT (vv. 4-5)

"Despiseth thou the riches of his goodness and forbearance and long-suffering, not knowing that the goodness of God leadeth thee to repentance? But after thy hardness and impenitent heart treasurest up unto thyself wrath against the day of wrath and revelation of the righteous judgment of God."

God is good to mankind. He leads people toward repentance, but they choose to move toward judgment instead. They pile up a storehouse of guilt that will cave in on them in judgment.

The Worst Sin

All sin is ultimately committed against God, and the most heinous crime of all against Him is to reject what He has done. All mankind is guilty of rejecting His goodness, abusing His mercy, ignoring His grace, spurning His love, and mocking His kindness.

Matthew Henry said in his commentary on Romans 2:4, "There is in every wilful sin an interpretative contempt of the goodness of God" (*Matthew Henry's Commentary on the Whole Bible*, vol. 6 [N.Y.: Revell, n.d.]). Whenever you or I sin, we show contempt for God's goodness. The book of Hosea records God's love for wayward Israel. In Hosea 11:1 God says, "When Israel was a child, then I loved him." Then He says, "I drew them with cords of a man, with bands of love; and I was to them as they that take off the yoke on their jaws, and I laid food before them. . . . and my people are bent to backsliding from me" (vv. 4, 7). With love, tenderness, graciousness, kindness, and mercy God reached out to draw Israel to Him, yet Israel drew away from Him.

A. God's Goodness (v. 4)

"Despiseth thou the riches of his goodness and forbearance and long-suffering, not knowing that the goodness of God leadeth thee to repentance?"

1. The devaluation of His goodness

The Greek word translated "despisest" means "to grossly underestimate the value or significance of something." It is the failure to assess true worth. Thus Paul uses it to describe people who make light of the riches of God's goodness. Despising mercy is the blackest of sins.

Every person on the face of the earth has personally experienced the goodness of God in many ways. The Lord causes the rain to fall on the just and the unjust (Matt. 5:45). He gives both the righteous and the unrighteous food to eat, fire to keep warm, and water to quench thirst. He gives us a blue sky, a warm sun, green grass, and beautiful mountains. He gives us people to love. God demonstrates His goodness in many ways.

2. The depth of His goodness

a) "Goodness" (Gk. *chrēstotēs*) is translated "kindness" in the *New American Standard Bible,* when Paul lists the fruit of the Spirit (Gal. 5:22). The word describes all God's benefits—His many kindnesses to mankind.

b) "Forbearance" (Gk., *anochē*) means truce, the cessation of hostilities, and the withholding of judgment.

c) "Long-suffering" (Gk., *makrothumia*) refers to patience. It depicts one who has the power to avenge but doesn't use it. It is a great characteristic of God. Scripture is replete with references to the patience of

God. He is patient with mankind because He doesn't want anyone to perish (2 Pet. 3:9).

For long periods God is kind and withholds His judgment. He is "slow to anger, and of great kindness" (Neh. 9:17). God isn't only good, forbearing, and long-suffering; He epitomizes those attributes. That great reality has been referred to as common grace or the providence of God.

3. The demonstration of His goodness

a) As seen in the psalms

(1) Psalm 52:1—"The goodness of God endureth continually."

(2) Psalm 119:68—"Thou art good, and doest good."

(3) Psalm 33:5—"The earth is full of the goodness of the Lord."

(4) Psalm 145:9—"His tender mercies are over all his works."

(5) Psalm 107:8—"Oh, that men would praise the Lord for his goodness."

b) As seen in the world

Sadly enough most people don't view God as good. They wonder how He can allow certain bad things to happen. They don't understand that God's goodness prevents man from falling over dead whenever he commits a sin. Because of the Fall of man, He has every right to wipe out the human race. Only because of His goodness, forbearance, and long-suffering are we able to keep breathing. It is a case of mercy rejoicing over judgment (James 2:13).

(1) The past

God was especially good to Israel. He was good to the pagans in Noah's time. He waited 120 years for them to repent while Noah preached righteousness (2 Pet. 2:5). He was patient with the nations (Acts 14:16). He overlooked their ignorance (Acts 17:30). He was so patient that He waited 700 years before judging Israel and 800 years before judging Judah.

(2) The present

God is wonderfully patient with us today even though people sin so greatly and so often. His divine law is trampled under foot. God Himself is openly despised, and His name is blasphemed. Yet amazingly He doesn't strike dead the people who blatantly sin against Him.

Why doesn't God cut people down when they sin, as He did Ananias and Sapphira? Why doesn't He cause the earth to open up and swallow us like Dathan and Abiram? What about apostates in Christendom and their toleration of every form of evil? How can He let that go on? Why doesn't the righteous wrath of heaven consume them? Indeed God has "endured with much long-suffering the vessels of wrath fitted to destruction" (Rom. 9:22).

4. The design of His goodness

a) Inspected

If you as a Christian have ever thought that God is unjust, you have revealed how easy it is to learn to abuse the goodness of God. The goodness of God is designed to lead men to repentance (Rom. 2:4), to cause us to turn from sin to Him, to long for Him and His goodness, and make us thankful He let us live in spite of our sin. If you recognize what you really deserve, you'll thank God continually that He doesn't strike you down. God's goodness and patience should lead us to repent with thankful hearts.

b) Rejected

But men despise God's goodness. Even Christians can be guilty of that sin. One commentator said that almost everyone has a vague and undefined hope of impunity and a feeling that bad things can't happen to him. The Jewish people believed that they were exempt from the judgment of God, and many people believe the same thing today. So they take advantage of God's goodness and providence. They enjoy the pleasures of life—the wonders of love, children, parents, friends, a spouse, beauty, fun, and all the delicacies of life from God—yet never offer a speck of repentance for their denial of God's glory.

It is terrible to be unthankful. Romans 1:21 condemns the heathen for failing to glorify God and for being unthankful. Nineteenth-century German poet and critic Heinrich Heine reportedly said on his deathbed, "God will pardon me. It is His trade" (Edmond and Charles Goncourt, *Journal*, 23 Feb. 1863). Many of us fall into that trap. Because we're so used to His mercy we continue to sin, figuring God will forgive us again—and again.

B. Ultimate Judgment (v. 5)

"After thy hardness and impenitent heart treasurest up unto thyself wrath against the day of wrath and revelation of the righteous judgment of God."

1. The problem

a) How people view themselves

Some people don't see God's nature as loving, good, and kind. They don't say, "O God, thank You for another day of life. Thank You for the partner I love. Thank You for not taking my life because of my sin." They take it all for granted, believing they're just getting what they deserve.

A great sickness has developed in contemporary evangelical Christianity that stems from focusing on self. The emphasis on self-image, self-esteem, and self-worth is nothing more than humanistic worldliness. Selfism has twisted evangelicalism from being God-centered to man-centered. Salvation is now seen from the viewpoint of what it can do for us. That is a horrifying error.

b) How people view God

People often see God as unjust. When one of our loved ones dies or is afflicted with a terrible disease, the first thought is often, *That's not fair. How could You do that, God?* We tend to question God's love and His acts.

(1) The wrong perspective

How can people question God's goodness? Because they see history from the wrong perspective.

(*a*) Lot's wife

As we look at the Old Testament we see that God turned Lot's wife into a pillar of salt because she looked back at Sodom and Gomorrah (Gen. 19:26). On the surface God's action appears to be arbitrary. People ask, "What kind of a God would dole out such cruel and whimsical punishment?"

(*b*) The Canaanites

God called for the extermination of every Canaanite. Concerning Babylon, Psalm 137:9 says: "Happy shall he be, that taketh and dasheth thy little ones against the stones." What kind of God would do that? Some people are so distressed by that statement that they conclude the God of the Old Testament is different from the God of the New.

(*c*) Aaron's sons

Aaron had two sons: Nadab and Abihu (Lev. 10:1). They had just been ordained as priests. Leviticus 10:1-2 says that they "took either of them his censer, and put fire therein, and put incense thereon, and offered strange fire before the Lord, which he commanded them not. And there went out fire from the Lord, and devoured them, and they died before the Lord." Can you imagine how Aaron felt? He may have thought, *God, they were just young men. They were merely excited about what they were doing. Couldn't You have just warned them not to be flippant about their ministry?*

(*d*) The Flood

How could God drown the whole world? It surely seems like cruel and unusual punishment.

(*e*) Capital punishment

There are nearly thirty-five sins listed in the Old Testament for which God prescribed the death penalty. They include such offenses as: hitting or cursing one's parents, murder, kidnapping, homosexuality, magic, violating the Sabbath, blasphemy, desecration, child sacrifice, contact with spiritualists, unlawful divorce, and false prophecy.

People view God as too severe. They complain that His punishment is arbitrary and whimsical. He doesn't always enforce the death penalty; He kills one person yet lets someone else live. The two young men did commit a foolish act, but they had to *die* because of it.

Lord Platt, writing to the *Times* of London about the *New English Bible*, said, "Perhaps, now that it is written in a language all can understand, the

Old Testament will be seen for what it is, an obscene chronicle of man's cruelty to man, or worse perhaps, his cruelty to woman, and of man's selfishness and cupidity, backed up by his appeal to his god; a horror story if ever there was one. It is to be hoped that it will at last be proscribed as totally inappropriate to the ethical instruction of school-children" (3 March 1970; cited by John W. Wenham, *The Goodness of God* [Downers Grove, Ill.: InterVarsity, 1974], pp. 7-8).

If you look at the Old Testament from a New Testament perspective, you'll get confused. We live under the goodness, mercy, and grace of God. Sometimes we think God is unjust because we compare His justice to His mercy, instead of comparing His mercy to His law.

(2) The right perspective

(*a*) God's original penalty was just

We cannot look at the Old Testament from the perspective of the New Testament; we have to start at the beginning. In the Garden of Eden God clearly warned Adam, saying, "In the day that thou eatest [the forbidden fruit] thou shalt surely die" (Gen. 2:17). Romans 6:23 says, "The wages of sin is death." Ezekiel 18:4 says, "The soul that sinneth, it shall die." At creation every sin was a capital offense.

God created man freely of His own choice. He made man to radiate His image and manifest His person. But man rebelled. Since God freely made man, giving him life and the conditions to continue that life, He has every right to take that life back if man chooses to violate His laws. Whenever we sin, we strike a blow at God's sovereign character and misrepresent His image and intention for us. If God takes back what He freely gave us because we violate His conditions, is that unfair? Of course not.

(*b*) God was merciful

Adam and Eve ate the forbidden fruit, but they didn't die. They didn't receive justice; they received mercy. But God required a substitute for Adam and Eve to satisfy His justice. Jesus Christ became that substitute.

Originally every sin required death. By the time the Mosaic law was instituted, only some thirty offenses required the death penalty. And even in some of those cases, there were times when God didn't enact His justice but spared the lives of the offenders. People were supposed to die when they committed adultery. Even though the Israelites were so adulterous, God permitted them to divorce as a gracious alternative. The people were also to die for idolatry, but God forgave them many times. He was also merciful when they committed fornication or murder—many times He exhibited patience. That is not cruel punishment but an amazing reduction in the severity of God's judgment.

If you compare the Old Testament with God's original standard, you'll see that the Old Testament is full of mercy. But we are so used to His grace and mercy that we abuse God's goodness. We think we can get away with our sin. Whenever He does do what is just, we think He's being unjust. That shows how confused we are. Who are we to despise His goodness? When God killed Ananias and Sapphira, people wondered how God could be so cruel. But they should have wondered how any in the congregation remained alive. They were all sinners.

(*c*) God has a right to judge

We so easily abuse His grace that if He didn't give us frequent examples of His justice, we would become even more debased. So God takes a life or severely judges someone periodically to illustrate what should happen to the rest of us who have become so accustomed to His mercy. If we didn't have examples of the consequence of sin, we would go on blissfully treading on His mercy.

i) 1 Corinthians 10:8, 11-12—Verse 8 refers to people who committed fornication. God took the life of twenty-three thousand of them. Verses 11-12 say, "All these things happened unto them for examples, and they are written for our admonition, upon whom the ends of the ages are come. Wherefore, let him that thinketh he standeth take heed lest he fall." God gives us those examples to show us what should happen to us and to foster an attitude of thanksgiving in our hearts. Every day we should thank God for being merciful to overlook our sins.

ii) Luke 13:1-5—"There were present at that season some that told him [Jesus] of the Galileans, whose blood Pilate had mingled with their sacrifices." Apparently some Galilean Jews came to the Temple to offer their sacrifices. As they did, Pilate's men entered the Temple and slaughtered them so that their blood actually mingled with the blood of their sacrifices. The people crowding around Jesus were not asking about Pilate's cruelty; they were questioning God's justice and how He could have allowed that to happen.

The text continues: "Jesus, answering, said unto them, Suppose ye that these Galileans were sinners above all the Galileans, because they suffered such things? I tell you, Nay. But, except ye repent, ye shall all likewise perish" (vv. 2-3). Jesus was saying that those Galileans weren't any worse than the people to whom He was speaking. The key issue was repentance. Unless they repented, they would die also. The Galilean Jews were examples. They received justice as an illustration of what would happen to all who didn't repent.

Jesus then gave another example of the same principle: "Or those eighteen, upon whom the tower in Siloam fell, and killed them, think ye that they were sinners above all men that dwelt in Jerusalem? I tell you, Nay. But, except ye repent, ye shall all likewise perish" (vv. 4-5).

History affirms God's goodness. He has appointed some individuals as examples to warn us of sin's consequences and to make us grateful that we haven't received justice.

2. The result

If you refuse to be led to repentance by God's goodness and if you will not thank Him and come to Christ, then your hard and unconverted heart is piling up wrath. You may be avoiding God's judgment now, but in the day when the fullness of wrath is revealed at the Great White Throne, God's righteous judgment will break loose upon you. Because God is merciful, people think their future is secure. Instead of being driven to repentance because God has been so kind to them as sinners, they are under the illusion that they have nothing to be concerned about. People may tread on His mercy now, but they will experience the fullness of His wrath one day.

a) The state of the heart

The Greek word translated "hardness" (*sklērotēs*) in Romans 2:5 gives us the English word *sclerosis*. It refers to the hardening of something, such as the arteries (arteriosclerosis). Hardening of the arteries may take you to the grave, but hardening of the heart will take you to hell.

Paul also referred to the heart that's "impenitent," which means "nonrepentant," "unconverted," or "unchanged." Ezekiel said that the Israelites had a stony heart (Ezek. 3:7; 36:26). Jesus also talked about people with hard hearts (Matt. 19:8; Mark 3:5; 6:52; 8:17; John 12:40). The writer of Hebrews urged his audience three times not to harden their hearts (Heb. 3:8, 15; 4:7). Those who become cold and indifferent store up wrath for themselves.

b) The time of the judgment

I believe that the "day of wrath and revelation of the righteous judgment of God" (Rom. 2:5) refers to the Great White Throne. Revelation 20:11-15 tells us that the Lord will call together all the wicked dead. They will be "judged out of those things which were written in the books, according to their works" (v. 12) and will then be cast forever into the lake of fire with the devil and his angels.

Conclusion

You can tread on God's mercy now and receive fury in the future, or you can recognize His mercy for what it is, be grateful, and come to God with a repentant heart and believe in Christ. If God's goodness to you is not leading you to repentance, then every sin you commit is filling up a reservoir of God's patience that is held together by His mercy. Someday it will get too full. When the dam breaks you will be drowned in an eternal flood of your own sins. But you have an alternative. In the midst of that flood is an island of safety: the island of Calvary, where the Savior waits for you to come to Him.

Focusing on the Facts

1. What can be characterized as the worst sin (see pp. 25-26)?
2. When we sin, what do we show contempt for (see p. 26)?
3. What do people despise about God (Rom. 2:4; see p. 26)?
4. Explain the depth of God's goodness (see pp. 26-27).

5. What don't most people in the world understand about God's goodness (see p. 27)?
6. How patient was God with Israel (see pp. 27-28)?
7. What is the design of God's goodness (see pp. 28-29)?
8. What do many people today believe about God's judgment (see p. 29)?
9. How do people see themselves in relation to the goodness of God (see p. 29)?
10. Of what do some people accuse God when things go wrong in life (see p. 30)?
11. Describe how some people view God based on His actions in the Old Testament (see pp. 30-32).
12. With what must we compare God's mercy (see p. 33)?
13. What was true of all sin in the beginning (see p. 33)?
14. What happened to Adam and Eve when they ate the forbidden fruit? What is significant about that (see p. 33)?
15. What is significant about the fact that there were only about thirty capital offenses when the Mosaic law was instituted (see p. 33)?
16. What is God's purpose in giving us examples of people who received judgment (see pp. 33-34)?
17. What is the point Jesus is making in Luke 13:2-5 (see pp. 34-35)?
18. What are people doing when they refuse to be led to repentance by God's goodness (Rom. 2:5; p. 35)?
19. How are those who reject God characterized (Rom. 2:5)? Explain (see pp. 35-36).

Pondering the Principles

1. Psalm 107:8 says, "Oh, that men would praise the Lord for his goodness." Do that right now. Examine your life and identify the obvious places where you have seen God's goodness at work. Then think of the many different kinds of sins you have committed. Thank God for His goodness in not giving you what you deserve. Finally thank God for the gift of relationships. Recognize that everything you have is the result of God's goodness.

2. Review the entire chapter. As you do, record the facts that would help you in a gospel presentation to those who question God's fairness in dealing with mankind. Next prepare an out-

line or small presentation of those truths. Ask God to direct you in your preparation. Ask Him to use your efforts in helping people to see the reality of God's goodness and how that leads to repentance from sin.

3
Principles of God's Judgment—Part 3

Outline

Introduction

Review

I. Knowledge (v. 1)
II. Truth (vv. 2-3)
III. Guilt (vv. 4-5)

Lesson

IV. Deeds (vv. 6-10)
- A. The Principle (v. 6)
  - 1. The role of works
    - *a*) In the Old Testament
    - *b*) In the New Testament
  - 2. The classes of people
  - 3. The facts about salvation
    - *a*) It is given by God
    - *b*) It is confirmed by works
- B. The Groups (vv. 7-10)
  - 1. Those who receive eternal life (vv. 7, 10)
    - *a*) Their active seeking of it (v. 7)
      - (1) "Glory"
      - (2) "Honor"
      - (3) "Immortality"
    - *b*) Their actual receiving of it (v. 10)
      - (1) The proof
      - (2) The recipients

2. Those who receive wrath (vv. 8-9)
   a) The unbeliever's rejection (v. 8*a*)
      (1) They are contentious
      (2) They don't obey the truth
      (3) They obey unrighteousness
   b) God's reaction (vv. 8*b*-9)
      (1) "Indignation"
      (2) "Wrath"
      (3) "Tribulation"
      (4) "Anguish"

Introduction

Hebrews 9:27 says, "It is appointed unto men once to die, but after this the judgment." Human history moves inexorably and unavoidably toward a final sentencing. The writer of Hebrews warned "of judgment and fiery indignation, which shall devour [God's] adversaries" (10:27). He also said, "Vengeance belongeth unto me, I will recompense, saith the Lord. And again, The Lord shall judge his people. It is a fearful thing to fall into the hands of the living God" (10:30-31). God will judge all mankind. Throughout Scripture He has warned us of that judgment to come.

A question of great importance now faces us. Since all people will face the judgment of God, what is to be the standard for that judgment? On what basis will some be condemned and sent to hell forever? And on what basis will some be sent to heaven forever?

Review

The apostle Paul gives the basis of God's judgment in Romans 2:1-16. There we find that God judges on the basis of knowledge, truth, guilt, deeds, impartiality, and motives.

Romans 2 cannot be isolated from the rest of the book of Romans; it must be viewed as part of a larger picture in which Paul presents the gospel of Jesus Christ. The Greek word translated "gospel" essentially means "good news." But before one can hear the good news, he must know the bad news. So in Romans 1:18–3:20 the news is all bad: man is sinful and immoral. Even at his highest ethical point he falls short of God's standard. Romans 3:19-20 says, "We know that whatever things the law saith, it saith to them who are under the law, that every mouth may be stopped, and all the world may become guilty before God. Therefore, by the deeds of the law there shall no flesh be justified in his sight; for by the law is the knowledge of sin." Romans 1:18–3:20 is a setup for the remainder of the book of Romans. Beginning with Romans 3:21 Paul describes how Christ saves man from his lost state.

Romans 1:18-32 is basically a condemnation of immoral men. Chapter 2 focuses on outwardly moral, religious, self-righteous men. But both types have the same fate: they are condemned.

I. KNOWLEDGE (v. 1; see pp. 10-15)

"Therefore, thou art inexcusable, O man, whosoever thou art that judgest; for wherein thou judgest another, thou condemnest thyself; for thou that judgest doest the same things."

II. TRUTH (vv. 2-3; see pp. 15-19)

"We are sure that the judgment of God is according to truth against them who commit such things. And thinkest thou this, O man, that judgest them who do such things, and doest the same, that thou shalt escape the judgment of God?"

III. GUILT (vv. 4-5; see pp. 25-36)

"Despiseth thou the riches of his goodness and forbearance and long suffering, not knowing that the goodness of God leadeth thee to repentance? But after thy hardness and impenitent heart treasurest up unto thyself wrath against the day of wrath and revelation of the righteous judgment of God."

Lesson

IV. DEEDS (vv. 6-10)

"Who will render to every man according to his deeds: to them who by patient continuance in well-doing seek for glory and honor and immortality, eternal life; but unto them that are contentious, and do not obey the truth, but obey unrighteousness, indignation and wrath, tribulation and anguish, upon every soul of man that doeth evil, of the Jew first, and also of the Greek; but glory, honor, and peace, to every man that worketh good, to the Jew first, and also to the Greek."

A. The Principle (v. 6)

1. The role of works

Revelation 20:12-13 twice informs us that God will judge men according to their works. That basic truth is also stated in Romans 2:6. It is not a new concept—it is affirmed throughout Scripture.

a) In the Old Testament

(1) Jeremiah 17:10—"I, the Lord, search the heart, I test the conscience, even to give every man according to his ways, and according to the fruit of his doings."

(2) Isaiah 3:10-11—"Say to the righteous, that it shall be well with them; for they shall eat the fruit of their doings. Woe unto the wicked! It shall be ill with him; for the reward of his hands shall be given him."

b) In the New Testament

(1) Matthew 16:27—"The Son of man shall come in the glory of his Father with his angels, and then he shall reward every man according to his works."

(2) 1 Corinthians 3:8, 12-15—"Every man shall receive his own reward according to his own labor. . . . If any man build upon this foundation gold, silver, precious stones, wood, hay, stubble—every man's work shall be made manifest; for the day shall declare it, because it shall be revealed by fire; and the fire shall test every man's work of what sort it is. If any man's work abide which he has built upon it, he shall receive a reward. If

any man's work shall be burned, he shall suffer loss; but he himself shall be saved, yet as by fire."

(3) 2 Corinthians 5:10—"We must all appear before the judgment seat of Christ, that everyone may receive the things done in his body, according to that he hath done, whether it be good or bad."

(4) Galatians 6:7-9—"Be not deceived, God is not mocked, for whatever a man soweth, that shall he also reap. For he that soweth to his flesh shall of the flesh reap corruption; but he that soweth to the Spirit shall of the Spirit reap life everlasting. And let us not be weary in well doing; for in due season we shall reap, if we faint not."

(5) Romans 14:12—"Every one of us shall give account of himself to God."

God does not judge us on the basis of our profession of faith. He does not judge the Jew on the basis of his Abrahamic heritage. He does not judge you on the basis of your identification with a church. Rather, He judges people by the product of their lives. Does a person's life manifest obedience to God? One's life pattern is an infallible index to character. In referring to false teachers Jesus said, "Ye shall know them by their fruits" (Matt. 7:16).

2. The classes of people

My grandfather used to say there are two classes of people in the world: the saints and the "ain'ts"! There *are* only two classes of people in the world: those who obey God and those who do not. None of us perfectly obeys God. But some people in the world don't obey Him at all, whereas others seek to obey Him. Every man will face an impartial Judge who has a comprehensive record of his deeds. That record will determine his eternal destiny.

I remember reading about a new publishing effort in children's books. Through computer printing, a company has designed a storybook series that can feature your child. You simply send in your child's name, the names of his friends, his school, the name of his teacher, and something about his likes and dislikes. With that information a story will be written with your child as the main character. Now that publisher writes a fairy tale, but God has a book about everyone's life that's true.

3. The facts about salvation

   a) It is given by God

   Some accuse me of teaching salvation by works. But I don't teach that because the Bible doesn't teach that.

   (1) Psalm 115:1—"Not unto us, O Lord, not unto us, but unto thy name give glory, for thy mercy."

   (2) Isaiah 48:11—God said, "For mine own sake, even for mine own sake, will I do it; for how should my name be polluted? And I will not give my glory unto another." God promises to fulfill His own promises and will not pass off that responsibility to anyone else. To maintain glory for Himself in His saving grace, there can be no salvation by man's own works.

   (3) Jeremiah 31:31-34—"The days come, saith the Lord, that I will make a new covenant with the house of Israel, and with the house of Judah, not according to the covenant that I made with their fathers in the day that I took them by the hand to bring them out of the land of Egypt, which, my covenant, they broke, although I was an husband unto them, saith the Lord. But this shall be the covenant that I will make with the house of Israel: After those days, saith the Lord, I will put my law in their inward parts, and write it in their hearts, and will be their God, and they shall be my people. And they shall teach no more every man his neighbor, and every man his brother, saying, Know the Lord; for they shall all know me, from the least of them unto the greatest of them, saith the Lord; for I will forgive their iniquity, and I

will remember their sin no more." The New Covenant is a covenant of mercy and grace extended to unworthy people.

(4) 1 Timothy 1:15-16—Paul said, "This is a faithful saying, and worthy of all acceptance, that Christ Jesus came into the world to save sinners, of whom I am chief. Nevertheless . . . I obtained mercy."

(5) Ephesians 2:8-9—"By grace are ye saved through faith, and that not of yourselves, it is the gift of God—not of works, lest any man should boast."

b) It is confirmed by works

We will be judged by our works, but we cannot be saved by our works. So how do works fit in? Although they cannot save us, works are an important part of our lives.

(1) Philippians 2:12-13—Paul said, "My beloved, as ye have always obeyed, not as in my presence only but now much more in my absence, work out your own salvation with fear and trembling. For it is God who worketh in you both to will and to do of His good pleasure."

(2) Ephesians 2:10—"We are his workmanship, created in Christ Jesus unto good works, which God hath before ordained that we should walk in them."

We cannot be saved by works, but we have been saved to do good works. Therefore when God judges, He will look at a man's works to determine whether salvation has indeed taken place. An unbeliever's works will reveal his unbelief. They will reveal the absence of God in his life because all his works will be unrighteous. Even when he tries to be righteous his works will turn out to be filthy rags (Isa. 64:6). The believer, however, by faith has been given the power of God to produce righteous works. They will clearly indicate his salvation.

God looks at a person's works. If He sees manifestations of righteousness in them, the person is regenerated. If He sees no such manifestation of righteousness, the person is unregenerate. Therefore God's final judgment can be rendered on the basis of works.

Understand that Paul is not referring to salvation in Romans 2:6, so don't get confused. He doesn't bring up the topic of salvation again until Romans 3:21. At this point he is dealing with one element of judgment.

What implications does the truth that God judges us by our works have for you? If there's nothing in your life to indicate righteousness, then righteousness isn't present in your life. Paul said, "If any man be in Christ, he is a new creation; old things are passed away; behold, all things are become new" (2 Cor. 5:17). With no manifestation of a new creation, there can be no salvation. There may be periods of time when we walk in disobedience, but a person whose life is barren of righteous deeds cannot claim to be redeemed. Jesus said, "He that is not with me is against me; and he that gathereth not with me scattereth abroad" (Matt. 12:30).

B. The Groups (vv. 7-10)

1. Those who receive eternal life (vv. 7, 10)

a) Their active seeking of it (v. 7)

"To them who by patient continuance in well-doing seek for glory and honor and immortality, eternal life."

(1) "Glory"

The highest and most wonderful goal of any believer is glory. He seeks to glorify God in the present and attain the glory of God in the future. He seeks to follow 1 Corinthians 10:31, which says, "Whatever ye do, do all to the glory of

God." To give glory to God basically means to manifest His essence or nature. The believer seeks to be a vehicle through which God's glory can be manifest.

An individual who has no desire to glorify God cannot be a Christian because the basic desire of a true believer is to glorify God. We look toward that future day when we will see Jesus Christ and be transformed into His image, radiating His marvelous glory for all eternity (1 John 3:1-2). The goal of a true Christian is to reflect God's glory. As a result his life will manifest a righteous pattern.

(2) "Honor"

In a sense, honor is the result of glory. One who reflects the glory of God receives divine honor. As Christians our desire should be to please God and to hear Him say, "Well done, good and faithful servant." As you seek to manifest the glory of God, pray also that God would honor and reward your faithfulness.

(3) "Immortality"

Ultimately we seek immortality (incorruption). The glory and honor we seek will become a reality when we become like Jesus Christ in the resurrection.

A believer has a heavenly perspective. The true objective of the saint is to live for that which is eternal. As Colossians 3:2 says, "Set your affections on things above."

Basically eternal life is the life of God in the soul of man forever. First John 5:20 says, "[Jesus Christ] is the true God, and eternal life." Possessing eternal life means having Jesus Christ live in you. Paul said, "I live; yet not I, but Christ liveth in me; and the life I now live in the flesh I live by the faith of the Son of God" (Gal. 2:20).

Eternal life is not a quantity of time but a quality of life. The life of God in the soul of man will always produce a righteous pattern. If you are a Christian and your life is presently characterized by unrighteousness, you are fighting against the very nature God created in you at salvation. Once Christ comes to live in you, God's life should begin to dominate. But we fight and resist it in our human sinfulness.

Commentator John Murray said, "Works without redemptive aspiration are dead works. Aspiration without good works is presumption" (*The Epistle to the Romans* [Grand Rapids: Eerdmans, 1959], p. 64). People whose aim is heavenward will be judged by the life God has produced in them. From the time of Adam, a true believer has patiently sought to do what is right.

b) Their actual receiving of it (v. 10)

"Glory, honor, and peace, to every man that worketh good, to the Jew first, and also to the Greek."

All that we seek we receive. We seek glory; God gives glory. We seek honor; He gives honor. And when we seek immortality, He gives peace—for when we enter into eternal holiness in the presence of God, the battle with our corruption will be over, and the result will be eternal peace.

(1) The proof

When God sends the righteous into eternal heaven and the unrighteous into eternal hell, those who enter heaven will have sought glory, honor, and immortality. Paul doesn't say they deserve it, but they will have had aspirations for what is heavenly and godly. They will receive the glory, honor, and peace of eternal life because they have done good deeds. If no good works are visible, then the person's alleged salvation obviously wasn't genuine. We will be rewarded for our deeds because they are the proof of the righteousness within us.

(2) The recipients

The reward applies to the Jew first and also to the Gentile. God will give heavenly and eternal blessing to both. The Jewish people thought the Gentiles would be shut out from God's blessings. Although that isn't true, the Jews were first in priority in the covenant and chronology since Christ came to them first, so Jewish believers will be rewarded first.

Along with their priority in salvation, the Jewish people also have the priority in judgment. Condemnation will be more severe for the Jew who rejects God's truth. Amos 3:2 says, "You [Israel] only have I known of all the families of the earth; therefore, I will punish you for all your iniquities." Israel's punishment will be the more severe because of the intimacy that nation had with God. There's no exemption from judgment for Jew or Gentile and no exemption for the moral or the immoral.

2. Those who receive wrath (vv. 8-9)

"Unto them that are contentious, and do not obey the truth, but obey unrighteousness, indignation and wrath, tribulation and anguish, upon every soul of man that doeth evil, of the Jew first, and also of the Greek."

a) The unbeliever's rejection (v. 8*a*)

(1) They are contentious

The Greek word translated "contentious" (*erithia*) was probably derived from the verb meaning "to act as a hireling" or "to work for pay." Here it refers to those with selfish, mercenary ambitions. An unrighteous person is wrapped up in what pleases him. Second Timothy 3:2 says that men will be lovers of their own selves. That is the basic problem of unregenerate man. Second Corinthians 5:15 says the Lord "died for all, that they who live should not henceforth live unto themselves."

Looking out for yourself leads to a contentious attitude toward the Lord.

(2) They don't obey the truth

When a person is self-seeking, he resists what God says. Although God speaks the truth, unregenerate man is not interested in what God says or wants. He wants only what he himself wants. Man rebels against God and quarrels with Him—a reflection of the egotism of sin.

(3) They obey unrighteousness

No man lives in a vacuum—he either does right or wrong. Out of rebellion comes disobedience and then dire sinfulness.

The road to hell is simply defined: a spirit of antagonism toward the lordship of Jesus Christ. Therefore the road to heaven must be the opposite: an attitude of submission to the lordship of Christ. God wants you to seek glory, honor, and immortality. Although we won't attain those things in this life, we are to have seeking hearts. And when we fail we should have an attitude of brokenness. Eternal life belongs to those who exhibit God's work in their hearts by living in obedience to the lordship of Christ. Those who refuse to do so are unregenerate and will experience God's wrath.

b) God's reaction (vv. 8*b*-9)

Sin is basically an attack on God and precipitates a holy reaction.

(1) "Indignation"

The root of the Greek word translated "indignation" means "to rush along," "to be in a hurry," or "to breathe violently." It was used from Homer throughout the centuries to refer to the rage that swells within man. It was used to describe Pharaoh's desire to kill Moses (Heb. 11:27), the rage of the angry crowd that wanted to throw Jesus off a cliff (Luke 4:28), and a riot in Ephesus (Acts 19:28). God's indignation will burst out like a consuming fire against those who oppose the lordship of Christ.

(2) "Wrath"

This is another term for anger. It speaks of reaching a pitch of fury. At this point mercy and grace have ended. God's tolerance ends in a swelling, furious, final anger.

(3) "Tribulation"

The Greek word (*thlipsis*) speaks of putting pressure on something or someone. In Acts 11:19 it refers to the crushing persecution endured by the early church. It is used of the struggles of the saints (Rom. 12:12), of Paul's persecution that nearly led to his death (2 Cor. 1:8), and of Christ's sufferings (Col. 1:24). It refers to affliction that results in personal suffering.

(4) "Anguish"

The Greek word translated "anguish" means "narrow"—referring to the narrowness or confinement of a place. Think of it this way: God is going to be angry. His fury will reach a feverish pitch. The result will be affliction in a narrow place. I can't think of a better definition of hell than that. That confinement produces unimaginable discomfort.

The New Testament describes hell as an everlasting punishment (Matt. 25:46), an everlasting fire (Matt. 25:41), a furnace of fire (Matt. 13:42, 50), a lake of fire (Rev. 20:15), fire and brimstone (Rev. 14:10), an unquenchable fire (Matt. 3:12), and a place of suffering (Matt. 10:28). It will be the final resting place for everyone whose life pattern is continually evil.

God judges according to deeds just as He judges according to guilt, truth, and knowledge. True righteousness produces true good deeds. Unrighteousness, no matter how religious it may try to appear, will produce only evil deeds. And God will judge all equally. There will be absolute equity in ultimate judgment.

How Can I Produce Good Works?

Now that you know that in order to avoid the eternal judgment of God you need to produce righteous works, how do you do that? Romans 3 says, "The righteousness of God apart from the law is manifested . . . even the righteousness of God which is by faith [in] Jesus Christ unto all and upon all them that believe . . . being justified freely by his grace through the redemption that is in Christ Jesus" (vv. 21-24).

The only way to produce righteous deeds is to possess the righteousness of Christ. The only way to possess the righteousness of Christ is to have faith in His redemptive work. Do you believe He died for your sins? Do you believe He rose again for your justification? Do you believe He is alive—even now interceding for you? Do you believe He will soon come back to complete the redemptive plan? If you believe all that and receive Christ into your life, He will enable you to produce righteous deeds. When the day of judgment occurs, God will see your righteous life and know that it could only be the product of the indwelling presence of the living Christ. Then you will experience eternal life in its fullest sense.

Focusing on the Facts

1. What is Paul's emphasis in Romans 1:18–3:20? What part does chapter 2 play in the overall picture (see pp. 40-41)?
2. Cite some scriptures that show that God judges men according to their works (see pp. 42-43).
3. What is an infallible index to character (see p. 43)?
4. Does the Bible teach salvation by works? Support your answer with Scripture (see pp. 44-45).
5. What is the purpose of works in a believer's life (see p. 45)?
6. What three things do believers actively seek? Explain each (see pp. 46-47).

7. What is the true objective of the saint (Col. 3:2; see p. 47)?
8. Define eternal life. What does it produce (see p. 47)?
9. What does the believer receive in return for what he has sought (Rom. 2:10; see p. 48)?
10. What is unique about the position the Jewish person holds both in regard to reward and judgment (see p. 49)?
11. What three things characterize those who seek to do evil (Rom. 2:8)? Explain each (see pp. 49-50).
12. What defines the road to hell? What defines the road to heaven (see p. 50)?
13. What four things characterize God's final reaction to sin (Rom. 2:8-9)? Explain each (see pp. 50-51).
14. How can one produce good works (see p. 52)?

Pondering the Principles

1. Read 2 Corinthians 5:17. What is true of every Christian? Read Ephesians 2:10 and Philippians 2:12-13. What should characterize every Christian? Do the actions of your life manifest that? Give specific examples. Are you currently doing anything that could give someone the wrong impression about where your allegiance lies? Ask God to help you turn from those things and live in obedience to Him.

2. Romans 2:7 says believers patiently seek glory, honor, and immortality. Is that true of you? Is your highest motivation reflected by 1 Corinthians 10:31: "Whether . . . you eat or drink or whatever you do, do all to the glory of God" (NASB*)? Begin today to apply that verse to everything you do. Before you start any new task or activity, ask yourself if it will bring God glory. If it won't, don't do it. That may be difficult at first, but as you faithfully seek to do that which will glorify God, God will reward your faithfulness.

* *New American Standard Bible.*

4
Principles of God's Judgment—Part 4

Outline

Introduction
A. God's Impartiality Described
B. God's Impartiality Defended

Review
I. Knowledge (v. 1)
II. Truth (vv. 2-3)
III. Guilt (vv. 4-5)
IV. Deeds (vv. 6-10)

Lesson
V. Impartiality (vv. 11-15)
- A. The General Principle (v. 11)
- B. The Specific Issues (vv. 12-15)
  - 1. Two groups (v. 12)
    - *a*) Those without the law
      - (1) Their description
      - (2) Their destiny
        - (*a*) The definition
        - (*b*) The degree
      - (3) Their defiance
    - *b*) Those with the law
  - 2. Two reactions (vv. 13-15)
    - *a*) The doers of the law are justified (v. 13)
      - (1) The business of the people
        - (*a*) The hearers
        - (*b*) The doers
      - (2) The deceit of the hearers
      - (3) The purpose of the law

b) The Gentiles are responsible (vv. 14-15)
(1) Creation
(2) Conduct
(*a*) Examples of man's good
(*b*) Laws dictating man's good
(*c*) The motive of man's good
(3) Conscience
(*a*) Intensifying one's conscience
(*b*) Scarring one's conscience
(4) Contemplation

VI. Motives (v. 16)

Conclusion

Introduction

A. God's Impartiality Described

Romans 2:11 says, "There is no respect of persons with God." That means God is impartial. He doesn't look at the person but at his conduct to see if it is righteous or unrighteous. The issue is not whether a person is poor or rich, Jew or Gentile, man or woman, educated or uneducated, wise or foolish. God's sentence is based strictly on our character as manifested by our deeds. He is impartial and cannot be bribed.

The phrase "respect of persons" is one word in the Greek text. It is a combination of the words translated "face" and "receive." Paul was saying that God doesn't receive a person's face. First Samuel 16:7 says, "Man looketh on the outward appearance, but the Lord looketh on the heart." God is not partial. Partiality is the sin of judging outward circumstances and not inward merit. To have respect for a person's appearance is to rule in favor of what you see on the surface rather than on what is true in the heart. Only an evil judge would so violate justice. God cannot and will not do that.

B. God's Impartiality Defended

1. Acts 10:34—Peter said, "Of a truth I perceive that God is no respecter of persons."

2. Galatians 2:6—"God accepteth no man's person."

3. Galatians 6:7-8—"Be not deceived, God is not mocked, for whatever a man soweth, that shall he also reap. For he that soweth to his flesh shall of the flesh reap corruption; but he that soweth to the Spirit shall of the Spirit reap life everlasting."

4. Ephesians 6:9—"Ye masters, do the same things unto [your servants], forbearing threatening, knowing that your Master also is in heaven; neither is there respect of persons with him." The same phrase is used in Colossians 3:25 and 1 Peter 1:17.

Review

I. KNOWLEDGE (v. 1; see pp. 10-15)

II. TRUTH (vv. 2-3; see pp. 15-19)

III. GUILT (vv. 4-5; see pp. 25-36)

IV. DEEDS (vv. 6-10; see pp. 41-52)

Lesson

V. IMPARTIALITY (vv. 11-15)

A. The General Principle (v. 11)

"There is no respect of persons with God."

God judges men by knowledge, truth, guilt, and deeds, and He does so absolutely without favoring anyone. His judgment is based only on the subjective reality of a person's faith in Christ and the objective confirmation of that faith in his works.

God is fair. He doesn't favor people, nor does He hold those who know little as responsible as those who know much. He deals fairly with everyone according to the light or knowledge they have.

B. The Specific Issues (vv. 12-15)

That raises this question: does God judge everyone the same? No.

1. Two groups (v. 12)

"As many as have sinned without law shall also perish without law; and as many as have sinned in the law shall be judged by the law."

If you didn't have exposure to God's revelation, you would be judged accordingly. If you did, you'll be judged as one who did. God will be utterly and absolutely fair. In the final eternal judgment, God will show His equity and impartiality by dealing with men according to the light they possessed.

a) Those without the law

(1) Their description

These are Gentiles who don't have the law of God—the Mosaic law. Paul didn't mean they are without any law or that they have no sense of right and wrong. They are without special revelation, which is the written Scripture. Will God judge them although they never had the law? Yes, but He will judge them by different standards than He will judge those who did.

(2) Their destiny

(*a*) The definition

Paul said that people without the law will "perish" (Gk., *apollumi,* "to destroy" or "put to death"). *Apollumi* is used of eternal death in Matthew 10:28 and Luke 4:34. It doesn't mean annihilation or unconscious existence. When something is *apollumi,* it is ruined so that it no longer can serve its intended purpose. All people were created to bring glory to God and have fellowship with Him. When people don't come to God, they are ruined for His intended purpose.

That truth is best illustrated in Revelation. In speaking of the doom of the Antichrist, John said, "The beast that thou sawest was, and is not, and shall ascend out of the bottomless pit, and go into perdition [a form of *apollumi*]" (Rev. 17:8). Verse 11 repeats the same thought. Twice John said that the beast would go into destruction. Revelation 19:20 tells us what that destruction is: "[The beast was] cast alive into a lake of fire burning with brimstone." *Apollumi* did not mean that the beast went out of existence; it meant he was sent into a living judgment. Revelation 20:10 informs us that he is still conscious there a thousand years later.

I bring this issue up because some people claim that Romans 2:12 teaches that unbelieving people who have never heard God's Word simply go out of existence. That is not what Paul was teaching. Rather, they are ruined for their intended purpose.

(*b*) The degree

Paul said they will perish "without law" (v. 12). That means their ruin will be commensurate with their lack of knowledge—it will not be as severe as it will be for those who were exposed to Scripture. Nonetheless they will still perish. They will find themselves in hell, but in a lesser degree than those who had the law.

(3) Their defiance

Verse 12 tells us why those without the law will perish: "as many as have sinned without law." Although they didn't have the law of God, they still sinned, and "the wages of sin is death" (Rom. 6:23). Man sins even when he doesn't have the written law of God. Within him resides a sin principle: he chooses a lifetime and a life-style of sinfulness. Knowledge of Scripture is not a precondition for sin—people will sin without it. They are guilty of sin against God and must be punished because they have no Savior.

b) Those with the law

Romans 2:12 introduces us to the second group: "As many as have sinned in the law shall be judged by the law." That refers to those who received the specially revealed Word of God from the law, the prophets, and the holy writings—the people of Israel and anyone attached to them who knew the truth of God. Today it refers to people who go to church and are exposed to the truth in a Christian environment. They will be judged according to the greater light and privilege they've received. Jesus pronounced woe on the cities of Chorazin, Bethsaida, and Capernaum because He performed miracles there and they didn't repent. He concluded that the day of judgment will be more tolerable for Tyre, Sidon, and Sodom than for them (Matt. 11:21-24). Why? Because they knew much more, so they would bear more responsibility.

Those who have the law will be judged by the law in the final judgment. God is fair. The most severe judgment is reserved for those who know the most yet reject it. That is why it is a fearful thing to be apostate—to know the truth and constantly turn your back on it. You would be better off never to have known the law than to know it and turn your back on it. God is fair to judge those with and without the law accordingly.

2. Two reactions (vv. 13-15)

a) The doers of the law are justified (v. 13)

"Not the hearers of the law are just before God, but the doers of the law shall be justified."

Paul went a step further in his argument, apparently realizing that the Jews might disagree with his argument, saying, "We have been the guardians of the law and the agents God has used to reveal the law. We have written, rewritten, and preserved it. We should have the higher honor, not the greater condemnation. We who have possessed the law should be protected from God's wrath." People today might say, "We've been going to church all our lives. We've tried to be religious. How can we be condemned?" Paul replied to that unspoken argument, "Not the hearers of the law are just before God, but the doers of the law."

(1) The business of the people

(*a*) The hearers

The Greek word translated "hearers" is not the usual word *akouō,* meaning "to hear," but the word *akroatai.* It is used specifically of pupils who hear—constant hearers educated in the law. Greek scholar Marvin R. Vincent had a good translation of it: "Those whose business is hearing" (*Word Studies in the New Testament,* vol. 3 [Grand Rapids: Eerdmans, 1980 reprint], p. 27). That's exactly what the Jewish people did in the synagogues: week after week they heard the law and had it explained to them. They were professional hearers.

(*b*) The doers

It is not those who hear who are justified but those who make it their business to obey the law. James warned us, saying, "Be ye doers of the word and not hearers only, deceiving your own selves" (James 1:22).

(2) The deceit of the hearers

God's law doesn't protect hearers from judgment. In fact the more they hear without obeying, the greater their judgment will be. Some people will come to the judgment and relate all the different times they heard God's Word preached or taught, thinking that will count for something. But all that will count for is greater condemnation.

(3) The purpose of the law

God requires perfect obedience, but no one can achieve that. Thus the law is meant to drive us to a point of desperation, where we turn to God for the power to do what we otherwise couldn't do. Hearing the law doesn't do any good unless you obey it. Otherwise your guilt is intensified because only the one who obeys is justified.

b) The Gentiles are responsible (vv. 14-15)

"When the Gentiles [Gk., *ethna*] who have not the law, do by nature the things contained in the law, these, having not the law, are a law unto themselves; who show the work of the law written in their hearts, their conscience also bearing witness, and their thoughts the meanwhile accusing or else excusing one another."

The Gentiles might also question Paul's argument, saying, "We never had the law. How can we be condemned for not obeying it?" Romans 4:15 says, "Where no law is, there is no transgression." Romans 5:13 says, "Until the law sin was in the world;

but sin is not imputed when there is no law." And Romans 7:7 says, "What shall we say then? Is the law sin? God forbid. Nay, I had not known sin but by the law." If those things are true, how can the Gentile be held responsible when he doesn't have the written law? For that matter, does God hold anyone responsible who has never heard the written law of God?

Romans 2:14-15 gives us the answer. People are responsible even if they haven't heard the written law because they obviously have a law within themselves as seen by their behavior, conscience, and thinking patterns. Scripture gives four reasons explaining why those who have never heard God's truth yet disobey it are lost.

(1) Creation

Romans 1:18 says, "The wrath of God is revealed from heaven against all ungodliness and all unrighteousness of men." God's wrath is revealed against all men whether they have the written law or not. Why? Because they "hold the truth in unrighteousness" (v. 18).

How do they hold the truth? Verses 19-20 says, "Because that which may be known of God is manifest in them; for God hath shown it unto them. For the invisible things of him from the creation of the world are clearly seen, being understood by the things that are made, even his eternal power and Godhead, so that they are without excuse." Anyone can look around him and know there is a God. He can perceive that God is supernatural—more powerful than any other being he knows. Thus he is responsible because he knows at least that much.

(2) Conduct

Romans 2:14 says, "When the Gentiles, who have not the law, do by nature the things contained in the law, these, having not the law, are a law unto themselves." They don't have an external written law, but they do have an internal law that manifests itself in their conduct.

Pagans naturally do things written in God's law without ever reading God's law. Their conduct proves they know what is right and wrong.

(*a*) Examples of man's good

Many pagans pay their debts. Many honor their parents. Many people who do not know Jesus Christ and have never read the Bible love their wives. Many wives love their husbands. Many care for their children, and many children care for their parents. Unbelievers believe it's wrong to kill. People who are not Christians feed the hungry and help the sick. Pagans tell the truth, seek justice, and struggle for equity. All those things reveal an internal human code of ethics that is law. We see that operate in our political justice system. We see it in humanitarianism. Sometimes those things are warped, but pagans in any society naturally do things that are in line with God's law.

(*b*) Laws dictating man's good

The Stoics, who were pagan philosophers, said that man broke certain laws operative in the universe at his own peril, such as laws of health and morality. They called these laws *phusis,* which means "nature." They said men were to live according to what is natural.

Mankind recognizes that there is a universal code of ethics. In fact man feels guilt when he violates that very code of ethics within him. He has a definite sense of right and wrong.

(*c*) The motive of man's good

Unregenerate people do relative human good, but they don't do good in terms of spiritual righteousness. Their good is not based on the right motive because nothing is truly good unless it is done for the glory of God. But they do good in a relative human sense. When they do that, they show the law of God at work within them. They do good in the right manner, if not for the right motive.

Cyrus did good (Ezra 1:1-4; 5:13-17). So did Darius (Ezra 6:12) and Artaxerxes (Ezra 7:11-26). Ezra even commended Artaxerxes for his good on behalf of God's people (vv. 27-28). The city clerk in Ephesus quieted the rioters (Acts 19:35-41). Romans of high standing protected Paul (Acts 23:12-30). Barbarians showed unusual kindness to victims of a shipwreck by building a fire to warm them (Acts 28:2).

Man is totally depraved in that he cannot do anything good that glorifies God apart from divine intervention. But he can do human good, which proves that a law within him directs him to what is good. Most people don't end up in prison although that doesn't mean man is basically good. He is depraved. But within him is a sense of right and wrong that keeps him from being as bad as he could be.

(3) Conscience

Romans 2:15 says, "[The Gentiles] show the work of the law written in their hearts, their conscience also bearing witness." Conscience simply means "co-knowledge." The etymology of the Greek, Latin, or English word is the same, meaning "to know along with." It refers to a person's inner sense of right and wrong—the moral consciousness that pronounces judgment on one's thoughts, attitudes, speech, and deeds.

(*a*) Intensifying one's conscience

Man's conscience responds to the internal norm. In the Christian it is intensified because he has not only that basic internal law, but he also has the law of Christ that excites the conscience even more. Paul listened to his conscience, saying, "My conscience . . . bearing me witness" (Rom. 9:1; cf. Acts 23:1; 24:16). He recognized when his conscience confirmed that he was doing right.

(*b*) Scarring one's conscience

i) The Christian

The Bible also suggests that one's conscience can become scarred. Scar tissue has no feeling. That's why Paul told the believer not to violate his conscience (Rom. 14:13-21). In those verses Paul discussed the issue of Christian liberty. He said that if a believer tells a weaker brother it is acceptable to do something, yet the conscience of that weaker brother leads him not to, then he shouldn't do it. Once a Christian develops a habit of violating his conscience, he will scar that which he needs to protect himself.

Leprosy exemplifies the danger of lack of feeling. In biblical times people believed leprosy was a disease that ate away one's extremities. Now we know that leprosy creates a deadening of sensation in certain areas. As a result untreated people afflicted with it tend to wear out their extremities because they can't feel the warning signals to keep from harming themselves.

ii) The non-Christian

Even unbelievers have consciences. But over a long period of time they tend to become dull. Yet I don't think that unbelief ever completely obliterates one's conscience—it persists in informing of right and wrong. Little children are good illustrations of the conscience at work. When they do something wrong and are confronted about it, most of them lie because they know what they did was wrong and they're afraid of the consequences of being caught.

(4) Contemplation

Romans 2:15 says, "Their thoughts the meanwhile accusing or else excusing one another." In each of us is the ability to contemplate or reason an action as right or wrong. For example, a person without Christ hears about someone who murdered a child. What is his reaction? Unless he's completely given over to evil, he's going to accuse the murderer. Punitive systems exist in society because men know right from wrong.

The way unbelievers deal with the good and bad in their own lives and in the lives of others indicates that the law of God is written on their hearts. If they live up to the light God has given them, I believe God will reveal to them the full light of Jesus Christ. That was what Paul implied when he said to the Athenians, "[Men] should seek the Lord, if perhaps they might feel after him, and find him, though he is not far from every one of us" (Acts 17:27). John 7:17 says, "If any man will do [God's] will, he shall know of the doctrine."

VI. MOTIVES (v. 16)

"In the day when God shall judge the secrets of men by Jesus Christ according to my gospel."

God will judge not only a man's deeds but also his reasons for doing them. People cannot falsify motives. Judgment will ultimately reach into the secret places of the heart.

A. 1 Chronicles 28:9—David said, "Thou, Solomon, my son, know thou the God of thy father, and serve him with a perfect heart and with a willing mind; for the Lord searcheth all hearts, and understandeth all the imaginations of the thoughts."

B. Psalm 139:1-12—"O Lord, thou hast searched me and known me. Thou knowest my downsitting and mine uprising; thou understandeth my thought afar off. Thou compassest my path and my lying down, and art acquainted with all my ways. For there is not a word in my tongue, but, lo, O Lord, thou knowest it altogether. Thou hast beset me behind and before, and laid thine hand upon me. Such knowledge is too wonderful for me; it is high, I cannot attain unto it. Whither shall I go from thy Spirit? Or whither shall I flee from thy presence? If I ascend up into heaven, thou art there; if I make my bed in Sheol, behold, thou art there. If I take the wings of the morning, and dwell in the uttermost parts of the sea, even there shall thy hand lead me, and thy right hand shall hold me. If I say, Surely the darkness shall cover me; even the night shall be light about me. Yea, the darkness hideth not from thee, but the night shineth as the day; the darkness and the light are both alike to thee."

C. Jeremiah 17:10—"I, the Lord, search the heart, I test the conscience, even to give every man according to his ways, and according to the fruit of his doings."

D. Matthew 6:4—"Thy Father, who seeth in secret, shall reward thee openly" (cf. vv. 6, 18).

Our innermost secrets may be hidden from human judgment, but they are not hidden from God. We will be judged for our motives. You act either for the glory of God or for the glory of man.

Conclusion

All those elements of God's judgment will come into play "in the day when God shall judge" (Rom. 2:16). That is the day of the great white throne judgment when all judgment is committed to Christ.

If you haven't dealt with your sin before that day—if you haven't confessed Jesus as Lord, accepted His sacrifice on your behalf, and His atonement and payment for your sin—then you are treasuring up "wrath against the day of wrath" (Rom. 2:5). Ultimately it will damn your soul—and don't think that you will "escape the judgment of God" (v. 3).

Focusing on the Facts

1. Explain the phrase "respect of persons." How does it apply to God (see pp. 57-58)?
2. Does God judge everyone the same? How does Romans 2:12 support your answer (see p. 58)?
3. Who are those "without the law" (Rom. 2:12; see p. 58)?
4. What do some claim Romans 2:12 teaches (see p. 59)?
5. Why do people without the law perish (see pp. 59-60)?
6. Who are the people "with the law" (Rom. 2:12; see p. 60)?
7. In what way might those with the law disagree with Paul's argument in Romans 2:12 (see p. 61)?
8. Who will be justified (Rom. 2:13)? Who won't be? Explain (see p. 62).
9. What is the purpose of the law (see p. 62)?
10. In what way might those without the law question Paul's argument in Romans 2:12 (see pp. 62-63)?
11. How does creation create responsibility to obey God for someone without the law (Rom. 1:18-20; see p. 63)?
12. How does the conduct of someone without the law hold him responsible (Rom. 2:14; see pp. 63-64)?
13. In what ways do men show they know right from wrong (see p. 64)?
14. How did the Stoics support the truth that man has a knowledge of right and wrong (see p. 64)?
15. Does man do good for the right motives? Explain (see pp. 64-65).
16. Define conscience. How does it work in a Christian (see pp. 65-66)?
17. How can the conscience of both a believer and an unbeliever become scarred (see pp. 66-67)?
18. How does the ability to evaluate another's behavior hold the person without the law responsible (see p. 67)?
19. God will judge not only a man's deeds, but also his __________ for __________ them (see p. 67).

Pondering the Principles

1. Read James 1:22-27. Would you characterize yourself as a hearer or a doer of God's Word? Explain. According to verse 25, how does one become a doer? What is the benefit of being a doer? Is that true of your life? What area of your life is most characterized by hearing and not doing? Begin to be obedient to God in that area. Ask God for guidance as you implement His truth in your life.

2. A common objection to the gospel is this: if Jesus is the only way to God, what happens to the native in Africa who's never heard of Him? Based on this lesson, how would you answer that question? Organize your thoughts and write them out. Use that to set up a presentation you could use to answer that common objection.

Scripture Index

Topical Index